RAMB

IN
MID WALES

Twelve walks in the old counties of Ceredigion, Meirionnydd, Montgomeryshire and Radnor.

by
LAURENCE MAIN

On the moors above Garreg-ddu Reservoir (Walk 10)

Published in England by
Thornhill Press
Cheltenham
MCMLXXXIX

ISBN 0 946328 242

PLEASE RESPECT THE COUNTRY CODE

Printed by Billing & Sons Ltd, Worcester.

CONTENTS

ACKNOWLEDGEMENTS

I wish to record my special thanks to David Bick, who provided me with information on the Red Dragon gold mine, to Janet Davies, who drove me to several of these walks, and to John Roberts, who took me to the 'Cerrig yr helfa' standing stones in the Dyfnant Forest.

THE AUTHOR

Laurence Main has lived in Meirionnydd since 1981. He serves as the voluntary Footpaths' Secretary of the Ramblers' Association in both Meirionnydd and Montgomeryshire.

INTRODUCTION

These rambles are intended to give the pedestrian tourist an introduction to the vast and varied countryside of Mid Wales. This is, perhaps, the best part of Wales for walking as it has superb scenery but it is relatively unknown and free from other than the discerning tourist. The coastline has cliffs and sandy beaches, while wide river estuaries indent it. Inland there are rugged mountains and high moorland plateaux, deep-cutting rivers and waterfalls, forests and lakes. So low is the population density that parts are a green desert, while when you do have the privilege of meeting a local, it is an opportunity to practise a few Welsh phrases. This is Wild Wales, where the visitor can benefit from the experience of being in a different land with its own distinctive culture. The twelve rambles in this book are shared equally between the old counties of Ceredigion, Meirionnydd, Montgomeryshire and Radnor.

The whole family can enjoy these walks. Do remember that Wales is a mountainous country, however, and that it can rain! Although none of these walks is a climb up a mountain, some do reach quite respectable heights (above 1500 feet). A gradient profile is given for each walk to indicate how strenuous it may be. Allow plenty of time for each walk (two miles an hour is a fairly average speed, but a young family might cover just one mile in an hour). The important thing is not to have to finish a walk in the dark, but just in case you do, carry a torch and batteries. Good walking boots are essential, as is an anorak with a hood to keep out the wind and rain. You may want to take off clothes as well as put them on, so it would be sensible to wear several layers, while shorts could be worn under tracksuit trousers. A rucksack will be needed to carry the spare clothing as well as plenty of food and drink and an emergency first-aid kit. Don't forget to carry the relevant Ordnance Survey map and a compass, and know how to use them. If in doubt, turn back the way you came.

Detailed maps provide all you need for navigation, but they are complemented by written directions which conveniently face each map. Each walk has a story to tell, while full details of how to locate the starts is given. All the walks are circular, except for the ramble along the cliffs between Aberystwyth and Borth, where each end of the walk is connected by both bus and train. All but three of the walks can be reached by public transport, but this is usually infrequent in Mid Wales, so do check the current timetable before setting out. Telephone 0267 233333 for information on buses in Ceredigion, while the number for Meirionnydd is 06338 38838. Bus information for both Radnor and Montgomeryshire is available on 0597 3711.

TOURIST INFORMATION

Wales Tourist Board, Mid Wales Regional Office,
Canolfan Owain Glyndŵr, Machynlleth, Powys, SY20 8EE.
Telephone: 0654 2401.

THE COUNTRY CODE

Enjoy the countryside and respect its life and work.
Guard against all risk of fire.
Fasten all gates.
Keep your dogs under close control.
Keep to public paths across farmland.
Use gates and stiles to cross fences, hedges and walls.
Leave livestock, crops and machinery alone.
Take your litter home.
Help to keep all water clean.
Protect wildlife, plants and trees.
Take special care on country roads.
Make no unnecessary noise.

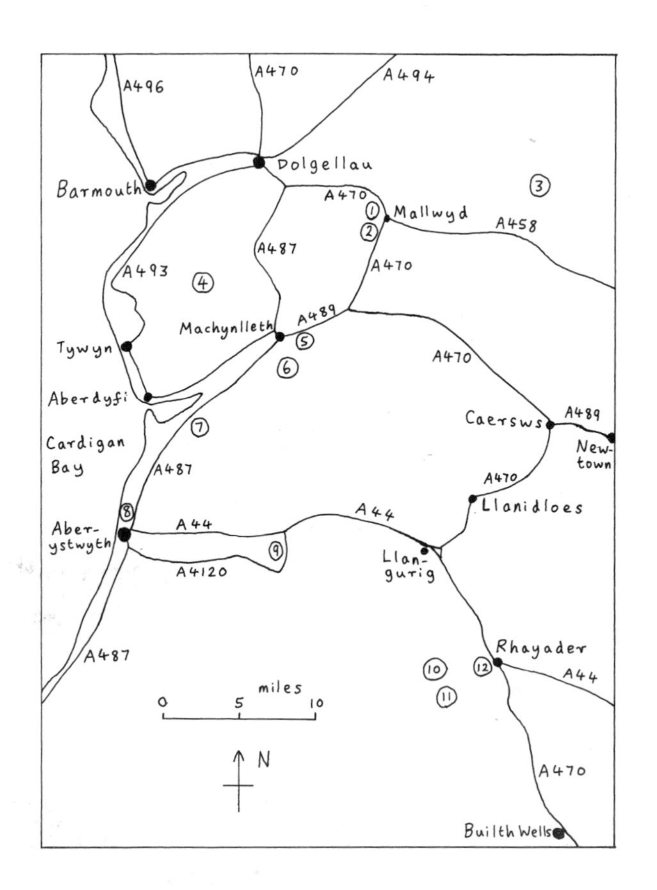

LOCATION OF THE WALKS

1 Red Dragon
2 Bwlch Cae-Tomen
3 Dyfnant Forest
4 Craig yr Aderyn
5 Henllan
6 Blaen-y-pant
7 Bedd Taliesin
8 Sarn Gynfelin
9 Ysbyty Cynfyn
10 Garreg-ddu Reservoir
11 Caban-coch Reservoir
12 Nant Gwynllyn

Looking down the valley of the Maesglase stream from Bwlch Siglen. The peak on the far central horizon is Aran Fawddwy (2971 ft).

1 RED DRAGON

Starting Point:	Layby on the A470 on your left just after Dinas Mawddwy, as you travel north towards Dolgellau.
Map Reference:	SH 856150 (O.S. Landranger sheet 124 or 125).
Distance:	4 miles.
Parking:	There is a layby at the start of this walk.
Public Transport:	There is an infrequent bus service to Dinas Mawddwy from both Machynlleth (S18) and Dolgellau (27).

This walk gives you a fine view of the waterfall down the crags of Maesglase.

Red Dragon is an old gold mine which was mislocated for years until a member of the Welsh Mines Society discovered an old estate map in 1984 (although the locals always knew where the mine was). Consequently it is still little known and a visit to it gathers the excited air of an expedition. This walk is enhanced by its gold mine, but it has so many other attractions that it would still be highly recommended if Red Dragon had remained lost. The first half of the walk, up to Bwlch Siglen, is part of Tony Drake's 'Cambrian Way' long distance route from Cardiff to Conwy. It climbs to reveal

Walk with the fence on your left on Bwlch Siglen.

splendid views up Cwm Cerist and across to the waterfall down the crags of Maesglase. The upper rim of the Dyfi Forest is encountered on Bwlch Siglen, but instead of taking the stiled path into the conifers on your left, you turn right to look down a beautiful valley with the dark peak of Aran Fawddwy on the horizon. The gold mine is at your feet, nearly five hundred feet down a steep path. Once in the valley, the mine can be found quite easily. The path passes an old ruin on your left and continues to a second, larger, ruin on your left, which housed the carpenter's and blacksmith's shops. Turn sharply left here to reach an old level near a tree. This was the gold mine, but don't be tempted in as the roof has collapsed after the first 150 yards. The ruins of the wheelpit and crusherhouse can be seen below the old level. The crushing machine was installed at a cost of £1050 in 1854, and was then found to be the wrong machine! The unfortunate venture ceased in 1856, having yielded very little gold. Slate was later quarried from the side of the valley on the right of your path.

Just before the valley path joins a road, an inscribed stone reads (in Welsh): 'Not far from Ty'n-y-Braich, on this road, stands the remains of Maesglasau, the home of Hugh Jones the hymn-writer 1749–1825.'

The carpenter's and blacksmith's shops, Red Dragon.

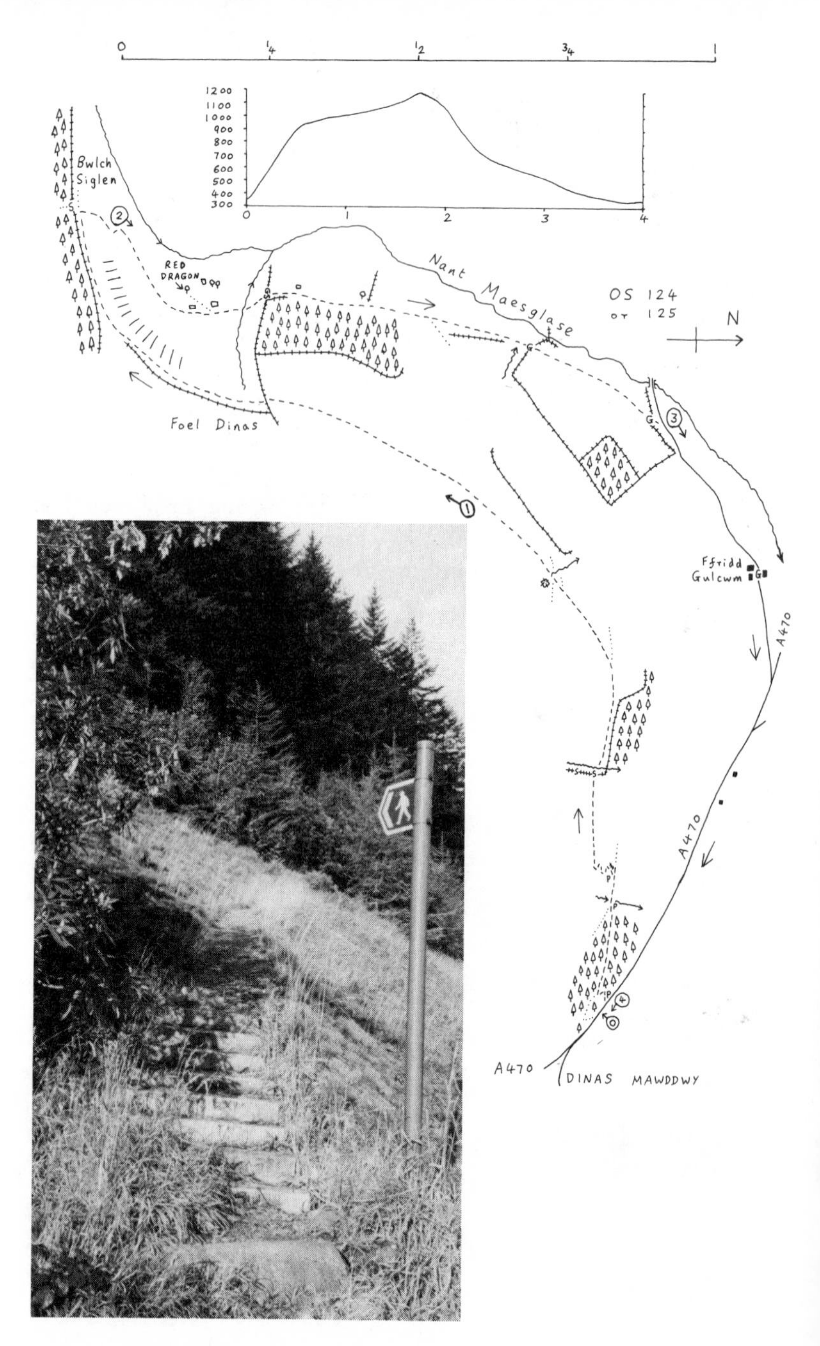

The start of the walk

WALK DIRECTIONS

Go up the steps which form the start of the signposted footpath on your left. This climbs quite steeply through the conifers, bearing right to reach a forest track at a signpost.

Go right along this forest track until another signpost directs you up a steep path on your left, which zigzags before bearing right uphill to a stile above a block of trees.

Cross the stile and a subsequent stream to walk with the trees on your right. The path is now fairly level, but avoid forking right down the bare hillside after the trees. Climb very gradually along the side of Foel Dinas at a height of about 1000 feet. Cross a fence (which isn't barbed) ahead to walk with another fence on your left to Bwlch Siglen, the pass which divides this valley from the Dyfi Forest.

Turn right to walk with the trees and the fence on your left on Bwlch Siglen until a stile on your left invites you to follow a dark path through the trees. Turn right here, however, to drop nearly 500 feet down a steep path to the floor of the valley.

Pass ruins on your left, the second of which is where you turn sharply left to visit the old Red Dragon gold mine. Returning to the main path, continue past the ruin of the old carpenter's and blacksmith's shops, cross the stream and reach a stile beside a gate ahead, with a conifer plantation going uphill on your right.

Keep to the clear, main track until it meets a road near the monument to Hugh Jones, who must have been inspired by the scenery of this valley. Maesglase, the 2213 ft mountain on your left, has the look of a holy hill and the valley beside it, down which flows a tributary of the stream which has been on your left, is called Cwm yr Eglwys. Eglwys is the Welsh for church and it seems that there was once a hermitage here and that this valley was owned by the old abbey at Strata Marcella, near Welshpool.

Bear right along the quiet, access road. When it reaches the busy A470, bear right along the wide, grassy verge back to the layby where you started.

2 BWLCH CAE-TOMEN

Starting Point:	Pont Mallwyd. This bridge over the river Dyfi is best approached from the crossroads at Mallwyd. Go down the lane opposite the A458. Mallwyd is at the junction of the A458, from Welshpool, and the A470.
Map Reference:	SH 858122 (O.S. Landranger sheet 124 or 125).
Distance:	3½ miles.
Parking:	There is space for roadside parking near the end of the lane from Mallwyd, near the bridge.
Public Transport:	There is an infrequent bus service to Mallwyd from both Machynlleth (S18) and Dolgellau (27).

The path up to Bron Camlan.

This is an exhilarating walk from the river Dyfi at Pont Mallwyd up to the crest of the ridge overlooking the beautiful Dyfi valley from the west. The route of the long distance 'Dyfi Valley Way' is followed into the conifers of the Dyfi Forest. A descent is then made along clear forest tracks which allow attractive views of the surrounding heights through the trees, giving the illusion of the Rockies, the Alps or of Norway. A narrow woodland path reminds you of Wales as it regains the ridge with its splendid views. It's downhill all the way back to Pont Mallwyd, which has a fine waterfall near it which used to provide the Buckley family at the old Plas in nearby Dinas Mawddwy with both salmon and ice, taken from the basin below the salmon leap.

This area, between Aberangell and Dinas Mawddwy, is where King Arthur fought his last battle. Bron-camlan is just one place name that refers to this. The dead were buried near Cefn-byriaeth and Bwlch Cae-Tomen, from where there is a fine view of Mallwyd church across the valley. This church was founded in the 6th century by St. Tydecho, a nephew of King Arthur. His less saintly cousin, Modred, was the traitor who died leading the rebels.

The view across the Dyfi valley to Mallwyd from Bwlch Cae-Tomen. Cross the ladder-stile in the fence as you descend.

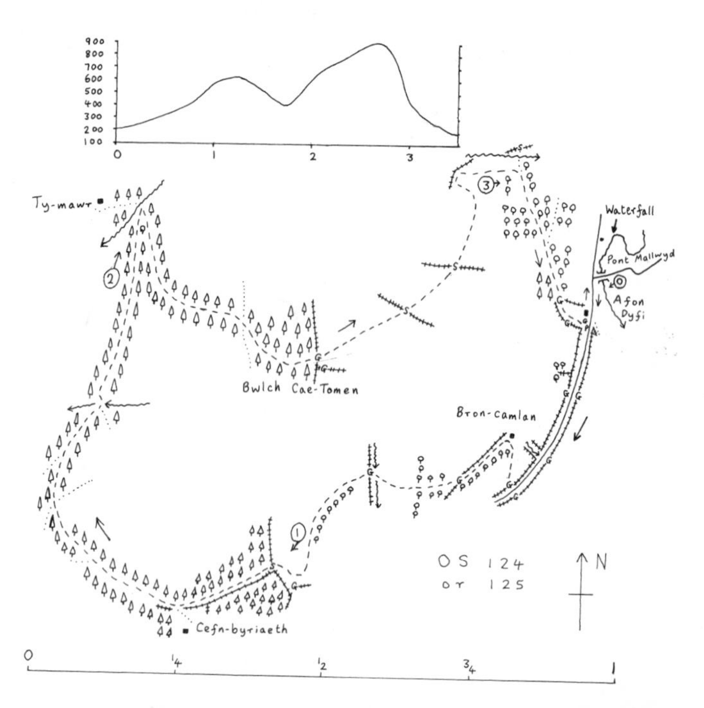

The waterfall near Pont Mallwyd.

WALK DIRECTIONS

Stand on Pont Mallwyd and look upstream. Take the lane on your left to walk upstream, with the river on your right, to see the waterfall. Go back to the bridge but pass it on your left as you climb up to Bryn-ffynnon. Continue past it and a gate with a public footpath signpost on your right. Walk along the lane until a gated path leads up to Bron-camlan on your right.

Turn left with the clear path at Bron-camlan and follow it uphill until a stile leads onto a path through the forest. Continue down a forest track at Cefn-byriaeth and ignore turnings until you reach a stream. Cross this and go ahead, climbing to another stream at a sharp bend.

Turn sharply right up a narrow woodland path, crossing a forest track to reach the ridge at a gate. Veer left downhill, crossing ladder-stiles, then turning right along a woodland path back to Bryn-ffynnon. Turn left down the lane to Pont Mallwyd.

Looking across the Dyfi valley to Foel Mallwyd from Bron-camlan.

3 DYFNANT FOREST

Starting Point:	Pont Llogel car park and picnic site, on the B4395, between Llangadfan and its junction with the B4393 (to Llanfyllin).
Map Reference:	SJ 032154 (O.S. Landranger sheet 125).
Distance:	9 miles.
Parking:	There is a car park at the picnic site.
Public Transport:	None.

Cerrig yr helfa, photographed by John Roberts in the spring of 1988, showing the upright standing stone which has since been knocked down.

This is a walk through a conifer forest. Sitka spruce is not as attractive as sessile oak, but the clear tracks of the Dyfnant Forest lead to an intriguing ancient monument. In 1956, trees were planted right up to a line of standing stones known locally as 'Cerrig yr helfa' but recorded in 1910 as the Bryn Bras Stones. When visited in 1910, there were six standing stones (the tallest was 6 feet, while the others were between 1½ and 2 feet high and each stone stood about 10 feet apart). A seventh stone was just visible in the bog. Now, however, 11 or 12 stones can be seen. This may be a result of the conifers draining the bog. The site was cleared of trees in 1988, but one of the stones was knocked over in the process. The ploughing may have deposited another stone on the surface away from the line, while quantities of quartz, which was probably brought especially to this site, can be seen.

Expecting a ley, or straight line, your author dowsed the stones. Instead, the dowsing rods led in a large circle. The extended line of stones does curve, so could there be a stone circle under the surface? A forester also noticed that the sun would rise in a notch at the summer solstice, with its rays passing through the middle of the stones. Taking a compass bearing, he walked westwards across the track and into the forest. His compass led to an isolated stone in the right position for an outlier sighting stone. It can be reached via a forest ride and is marked by big question marks painted on trees.

A local farmer, John Roberts, takes a great interest in these stones and has photographs showing the damaged stone standing upright, so it can be re-erected accurately. As the stones aren't marked on the O.S. map, it was a chance meeting with John that led your author to these stones and to the authorities subsequently being notified about the damage done to them. It just happened that one of the author's photographs of the stones (frame no 17 of a 24 frame film) was torn (the film was wound automatically).

Efforts are being made to have these stones protected from further damage as a result of the planting of alien conifers on this sacred spot. It is hoped to grass the area and to make it more accessible. It may even be marked on the map!

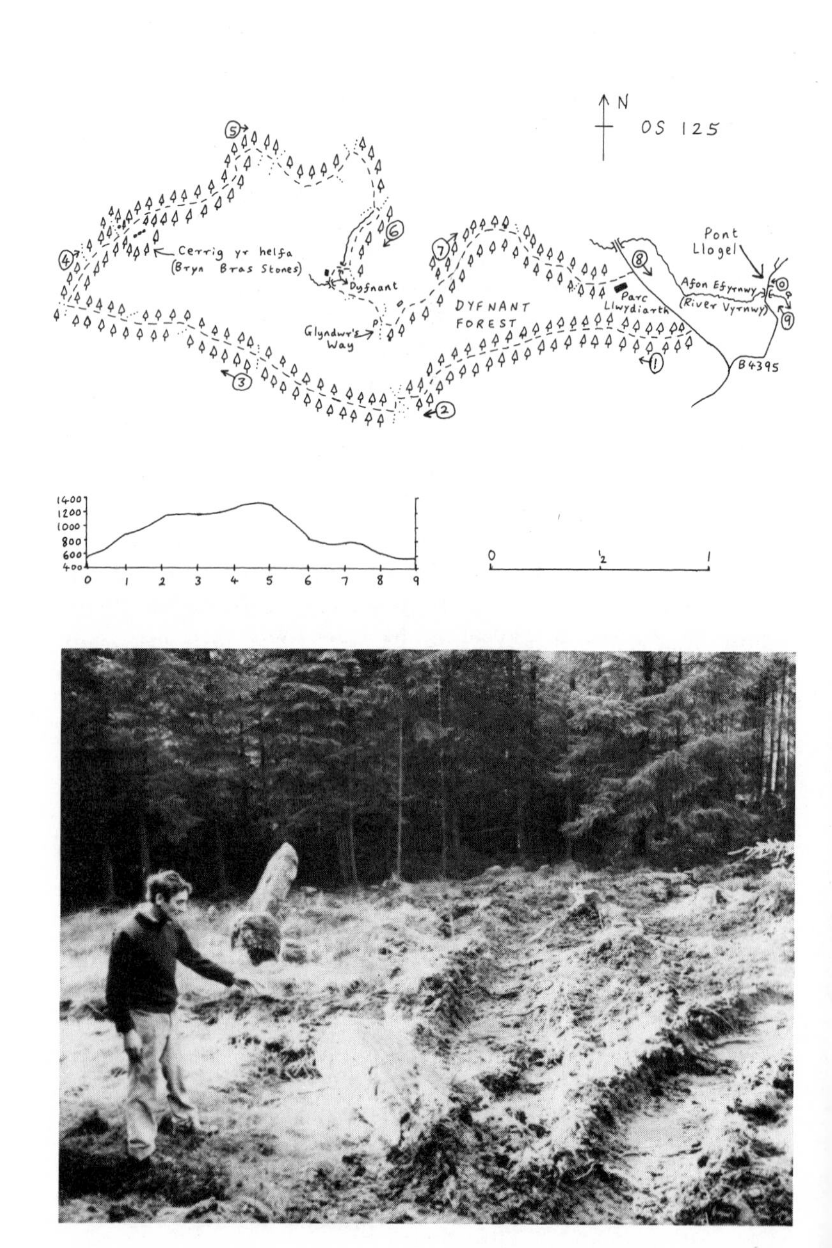

John Roberts points to the stone that was knocked down and damaged in 1988. It could have been erected over 4000 years ago.

WALK DIRECTIONS

Turn left from the car park across the bridge and walk south along the B4395 until its junction with a minor road on your right. Go right up this road until a forest track on your left.

Turn left along this clear forest track. Walk westwards along it for a mile to reach a junction of five tracks. Go ahead along the second track from your left. Turn right when it joins another track. Walk in a west-north-west direction for two miles, with another clear track joining yours at a sharp angle from the right.

Reach a junction with another clear track coming at nearly a right angle from the right and opposite a less distinct bridleway. Turn right up this track. Keep right at a fork just before an old quarry on your left. Look for the row of standing stones in a clearing on your right. The sighting stone is in the trees on your left (to reach it, go back a few yards, then up a forest ride until you see painted question marks on the trees on your right and the stone at their feet).

Go on past the row of standing stones on your right. This clear track reaches a height of 1358 feet before descending to a stream. Ignore turnings to right and left and keep to the main track as it contours round a hill on your left. Pass a track on your right and ignore two tracks on your left as you turn right downhill beside a stream. The track crosses this stream to put it on your left.

Follow the main track as it turns left across the stream, then immediately right to go downstream. Fork right across the stream again and pass buildings on your right before bearing left with the track across another stream. Keep to the main track, with the meadow on your left and trees on your right, crossing the signposted 'Glyndŵr's Way' before your track bends sharply left. Your track passes above a ruin in the meadow on your left before going through the trees to the edge of the forest.

Pass the buildings of Parc Llwydiarth on your right to reach the road. Turn right along this road back to its junction with the B4395 and retrace your steps to the car park at Pont Llogel.

4 CRAIG YR ADERYN

Starting Point:	The Talyllyn Railway's Abergynolwyn station, just off the B4405 on your left as you go from Abergynolwyn (½ mile north-east) to Tywyn (7 miles south-west).
Map Reference:	SH 671064 (O.S. Landranger sheet 124).
Distance:	5⅔ miles.
Parking:	There is a car park near the station.
Public Transport:	The seasonal steam train service on the Talyllyn Railway from Tywyn is highly recommended. There is a regular weekday bus service (30) between Tywyn and Minffordd via Abergynolwyn.

A steam train on the Talyllyn Railway near the end of this walk.

Travel in style to this walk on the Talyllyn Railway. The Talyllyn became famous when it was the first railway in the country to be saved by the enthusiasm of volunteers. It was opened in 1866 to carry slate from the quarries above Abergynolwyn to Tywyn, but it soon opened its 2 ft 3 in gauge tracks to passenger traffic. The closure of Bryn Eglwys slate quarry threatened the existence of the line in 1947, but a Talyllyn Railway Preservation Society was formed with the support of the last private owner, Sir Haydn Jones, and took over the running of the railway on Sir Haydn's death in 1950.

The highpoint of this ramble is more arduous, but the steep climb to the 762 ft summit of Craig yr Aderyn (Birds' Rock) is well worth the effort. The view inland to Cadair Idris explains why the 2928 ft mountain is described in Welsh as the chair of Idris (a legendary giant). This massive rock earns its name by having cormorants nesting on its crags. These birds normally make their nests along the coast, and they can be seen commuting the 5 miles from this rock to the sea between March and July. Craig yr Aderyn looks like a sea cliff and that is what it used to be at a time when this valley was an arm of the sea.

The walk up the Dysyni Gorge also offers magnificent scenery. A distinctive feature is Cow Rock, where iron rings can be seen set into a rock, with troughs cut into the stone. The farmer used to use these rings to tie up his cows when he wanted to feed them and milk them without the bother of driving them to his farm.

Abergynolwyn was built to house the slate quarry workers in the mid 19th century. It is situated close to the confluence of the Afon Dysyni and Nant Gwernol. A frothy whirlpool used to exist at this confluence and Abergynolwyn is named after it (Aber means the mouth of a river, while Gwyn olwyn means white wheel, or whirl pool). The Railway Inn serves real ale, while Hilary's Kitchen serves wholefood meals. Refreshments are also available at the Talyllyn Railway's Abergynolwyn station.

Even if you don't come here by train, acquire a Talyllyn Railway timetable and try to reach the level crossing in time to see the up train from Tywyn going to the terminus at Nant Gwernol. You should then have time to reach Abergynolwyn station for the same train as it goes back down to Tywyn.

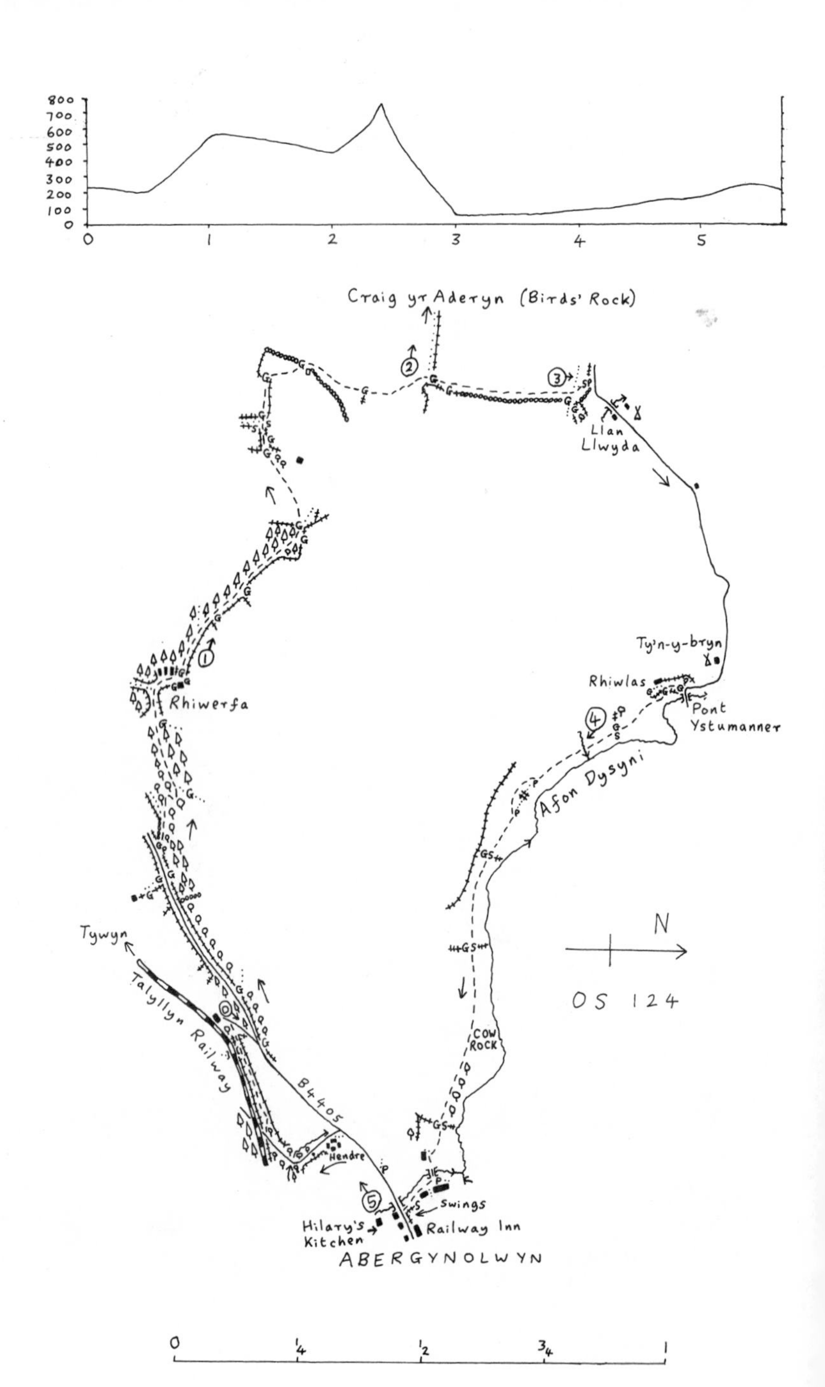
800
700
600
500
400
300
200
100
0
0
1
2
3
4
5
Craig yr Aderyn (Birds' Rock)
Llan Llwyda
Rhiwerfa
Ty'n-y-bryn
Rhiwlas
Pont Ystumanner
Afon Dysyni
N
OS 124
Tywyn
Talyllyn Railway
B4405
COW ROCK
Hendre
Swings
Hilary's Kitchen
Railway Inn
ABERGYNOLWYN
0
1/4
1/2
3/4
1

WALK DIRECTIONS

Walk downhill from the Talyllyn Railway's Abergynolwyn station to the main road and turn left along it until a signpost beside the third gate on your right. Bear right along the uphill track, ignoring a footpath on your left to zigzag through the oak trees.

Join a forestry track on the top and bear left along the main track to reach farm buildings. Turn left through the gate opposite the farmhouse to walk with conifer trees on your left and a fence on your right.

Go through a gate across the track and fork left along the higher track across open country. Continue along a gated fenced track, ignoring a turning on your left. Go ahead with a fence on your right, go through a gate and veer right to a gate in a stone wall.

Follow the clear path which bears right to another gate and go ahead to the foot of a fence which runs up the hillside on your left. Before going through the gate at the foot of this fence, divert up the well-defined path to the 762 ft summit of Craig yr Aderyn (Birds' Rock) on your left.

Having returned to the gate at the foot of the fence which runs up the side of Craig yr Aderyn, go through it to walk downhill with a wall on your right. Drop down to a lane ahead, crossing a ladder stile beside a public footpath signpost.

Turn right along this lane and walk along it for nearly a mile, until a bridge over a river (Afon Dysyni). Instead of crossing the bridge, turn right through a gate to follow the signposted path up the Dysyni Gorge, with the river on your left. Take care to follow a waymarked diversion around a dangerously eroded section of the original path and look out for Cow Rock, with its iron rings on your left.

Bear left at a building to cross a stream (Nant Gwernol) by a footbridge and reach the village of Abergynolwyn. Turn right to walk with Nant Gwernol on your right and houses on your left. Turn right at the main road, then go up the first lane on your left to reach the Talyllyn Railway. Turn right along the signposted path to Aberygynolwyn station, keeping the railway on your left.

5 HENLLAN

Starting Point:	Felin Crewi, a working water mill and café just off the A489 at Penegoes, two miles east of Machynlleth (look for its sign on your right as you come from Machynlleth).
Map Reference:	SH 774008 (O.S. Landranger sheet 135).
Distance:	5¾ miles.
Parking:	There is a car park at Felin Crewi.
Public Transport:	There is a regular weekday bus service (S22 or S18) to Penegoes from Machynlleth.

Felin Crewi

It is a risk beginning at Felin Crewi, because you may end up sampling all the wholesome, nutritious food and forgetting to go up the track leading south to cross the ridge into the next valley. Come early in the morning then, when it's easier to summon the courage for the initial climb and when you know there will be a good lunch in store at the end of the walk.

The walk is not strenuous and it does give you many attractive views. There are patches of the native deciduous woodland, so the autumn is a colourful time here. Sheep pastures and conifer plantations complete the familiar Welsh valley scene, with the sense of peace predominant.

This land was not always so peaceful. Around 1400, Owain Glyndŵr, the last independent, native prince of Wales, marched this way. Machynlleth was the scene of a Parliament called by Glyndŵr 'in the fourth year of the reign', in 1404. Powys County Council have initiated a long distance walking route called 'Glyndŵr's Way', which goes from Knighton to Welshpool via Machynlleth. It is 120 miles long and you walk about two miles of it to Forge.

An old millstone near the mill pond at Felin Crewi.

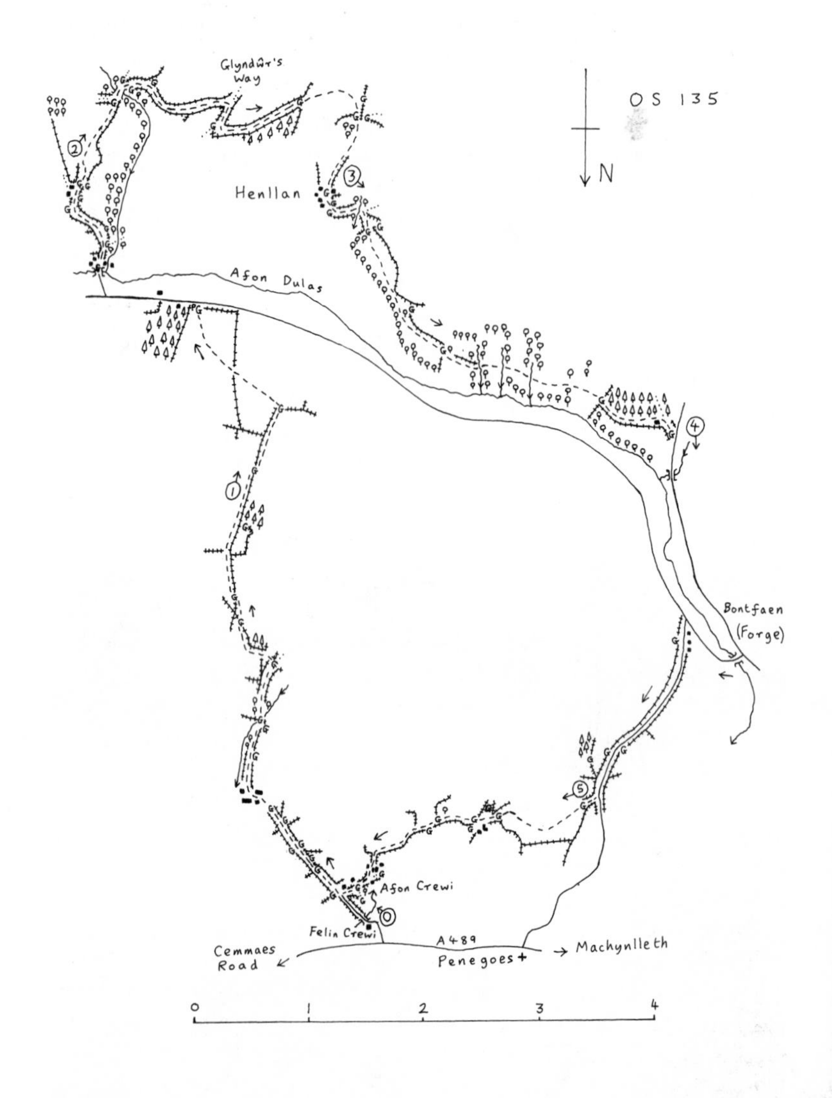

Glyndŵr's Way
OS 135
N
Henllan
Afon Dulas
Bontfaen
(Forge)
Afon Crewi
Felin Crewi
A489
Cemmaes Road
Penegoes
Machynlleth
0
1
2
3
4

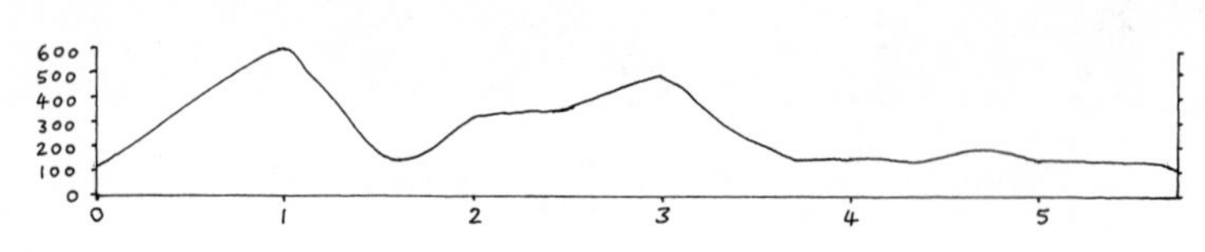

600
500
400
300
200
100
0
0
1
2
3
4
5

WALK DIRECTIONS

Go south from Felin Crewi across the bridge over the Afon Crewi and up the track. Continue through a farmyard to reach a gate across the track. Go ahead to a second gate, but turn left to walk with a small conifer plantation on your right. Bear right with the fence to a gate, which you go through to put the fence on your left. Go through another gate to walk uphill with the fence on your right again. Pass trees on your right on the summit and switch sides again by going through a small gate in the fence. Walk with the fence on your left down to a gate in the corner and veer left downhill to a gate beside a signpost in the far bottom corner of this field to reach a road.

Go left along this road until a lane on your right leads you down to a bridge across the Afon Dulas. Keep to the clear track through two farmyards and go ahead through a gate to follow the path across a field to a gate which gives access to an old lane.

Turn right to cross the bridge over a stream and follow this old hedged lane to a junction where it meets the waymarked 'Glyndŵr's Way'. Go right and bend left with the lane until a gate across it. Continue along the clear track which bends right to a waymarked gate and down to farm (Henllan).

Bear left with the waymarked track after Henllan and follow it as it runs parallel to and above the Afon Dulas until a gate into a conifer plantation. Go ahead with the trees on your left and go right when you join a track from your left to go down to the road.

Turn right along the road to Forge, where you turn right across the bridge over the river and bend right, passing the telephone box. Turn sharply left after some houses to follow a lane. Notice a small plantation of trees on your right and look for a track going right from the lane shortly after it. Follow this track to a gate and continue along it across an open field.

Go through a gate to pass a farm on your left and continue through a gate to walk with a fence and a distant view of Felin Crewi on your left. Look for a narrow path near the corner of the third field and follow it left to an old farm. Turn right along the track to your outward track. Turn left for Felin Crewi.

6 BLAEN-Y-PANT

Starting Point:	Go south from Machynlleth through Forge and along the access road to Talbontdrain, Uwchygarreg. Look for a layby on your right, just after Isybryn (on your left) and just before a signposted junction to Blaen-y-pant.
Map Reference:	SN 770980 (O.S. Landranger sheet 135).
Distance:	4 miles.
Parking:	There is a layby at the start. Don't obstruct any gates. Park considerately on a narrow road.
Public Transport:	None (but Machynlleth is only 2½ miles away).

Walking south along 'Glyndŵr's Way'.

Good, clear tracks, bare hillsides, afforested valleys and old green lanes all feature in this walk. It is probably the varied views that will be best remembered, for this is an upland walk in a quintessentially unspoilt part of Montgomeryshire.

Two sorts of waymarks aid navigation. Yellow arrows point the way along a section of 'Glyndŵr's Way', while Scots pines waymark old drovers' routes and places which offered the drovers hospitality. Until the coming of the railway, cattle droving was important to the Welsh economy. The famous Welsh black cattle were driven over mountains to England. Corgis were used to control the herds, while the dogs would find their own way home before their masters. It took three weeks to drive cattle from North Wales to Kent.

'Glyndŵr's Way' follows old drove roads on its 120 mile route across Powys. Its association with the great Welsh patriot is tenuous in places but this really is Glyndŵr country. The social discontent of the late 14th century manifested itself as nationalism in Wales and Glyndŵr raised his standard on nearby Pumlumon in the summer of 1401.

Scots pines line 'Glyndŵr's Way'.

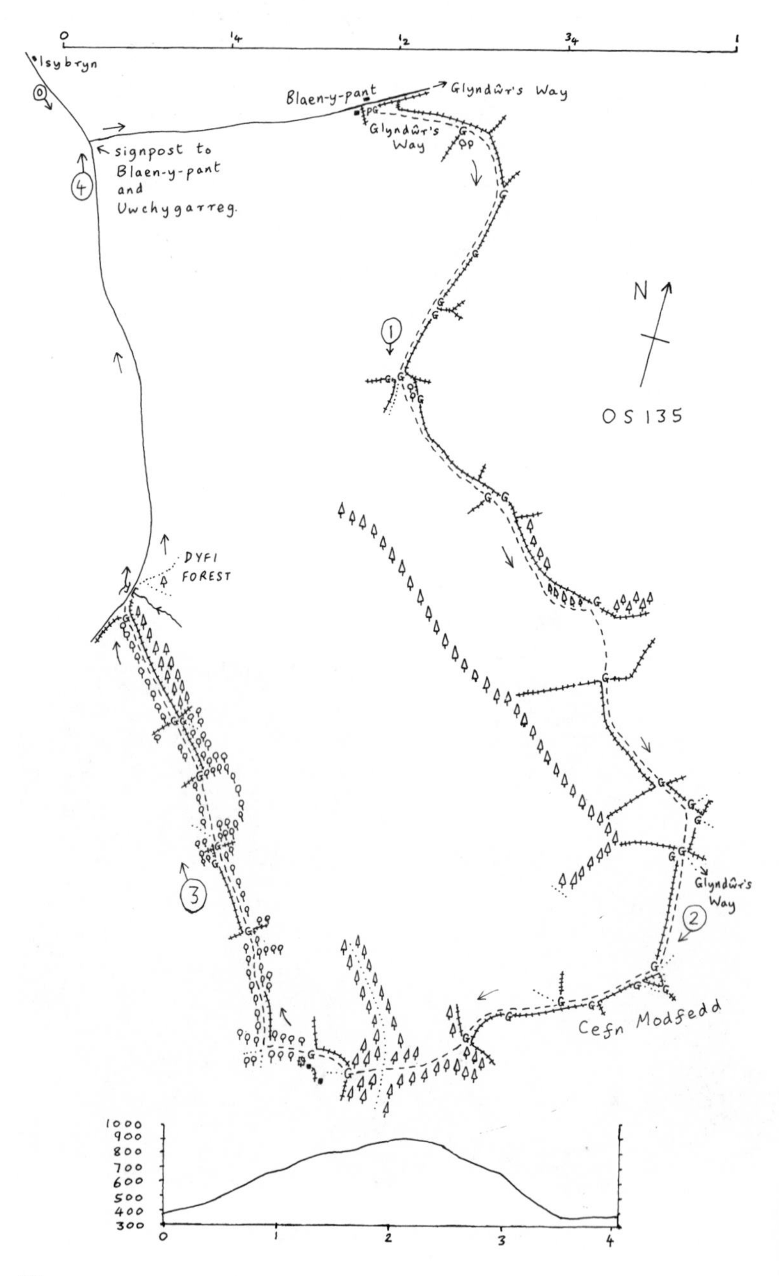
0
1/4
1/2
3/4
1
Isybryn
0
Blaen-y-pant
Glyndŵr's Way
PG
Glyndŵr's Way
signpost to Blaen-y-pant and Uwchygarreg.
4
N
1
OS 135
DYFI FOREST
3
Glyndŵr's Way
2
Cefn Modfedd
1000
900
800
700
600
500
400
300
0
1
2
3
4

WALK DIRECTIONS

Walk south from the layby to a road junction where a signpost with two arms points to Blaen-y-pant and to Uwchygarreg. Turn left to Blaen-y-pant, where you leave the road at a signpost on your right beside a waymarked route for over a mile along a clear track which climbs to an impressive height.

Leave the waymarked 'Glyndŵr's Way' when it goes downhill on your left. Go ahead with a fence on your right to join a clear track which descends with a fence on your left to a gate into forest. Go ahead, crossing a forestry track, to another gate onto open land and descend past buildings on your left to a crosstracks.

Turn right along an old green lane, which is delightfully shaded by trees. When you reach a road, turn right to pass the entrance to part of the Dyfi Forest on your right and continue to the road junction with its signpost. Retrace your steps to the layby.

Looking north-west from Cefn Modfedd.

7 BEDD TALIESIN

Starting Point:	Yr Hen Gapel (Old Chapel Museum), Tre'r-ddôl, on the A487 between Aberystwyth and Machynlleth.
Map Reference:	SN 661924 (O.S. Landranger sheet 135).
Distance:	4 miles.
Parking:	By the wall of the Old Chapel Museum.
Public Transport:	There is a regular weekday bus service (S14) to Tre'r-ddôl from Machynlleth and Aberystwyth.

Looking across the Dyfi estuary from Bedd Taliesin.

Wales is a land of mystery and magic, of songs and poetry. It is also a land of chapels, and this walk begins at the Old Chapel Museum, part of the National Museum of Wales and administered by the Welsh Folk Museum. This is open from 10 to 5 on weekdays from April to September, while the Cletwr Garage opposite it has a café which is open every day of the week all year round. Save these attractions for after the walk, however, for our goal is Bedd Taliesin, the grave of Taliesin, the Chief of Bards. Not that there isn't a connection between Taliesin and the Old Chapel Museum, for Christianity was the established religion of Britain when the Romans were still feeding Christians to the lions and the druids accepted Jesus as bringing a more perfect revelation of the faith. It was Taliesin who declared: 'Christ, the Word from the beginning, was from the beginning our teacher, and we never lost His teaching. Christianity was a new thing in Asia, but there never was a time when the Druids of Britain held not its doctrines'.

Taliesin lived in the 6th century A.D. and was a contemporary of King Arthur. He may have been the same person as Merlin, indeed both Merlin and Taliesin might have been titles. 'Johannes the diviner was I called, and Merddin'. According to legend, Taliesin began as little Gwion who, set to stir Ceridwen's cauldron, accidentally swallowed three drops of its brew and became inspired. Ceridwen vengefully pursued him and after much shape-shifting on both sides he hid in a wheat-grain, but she found and ate him. Later she bore him, a helpless babe, and tossed him into the Dyfi estuary in a coracle. Floating to the weir of Gwyddno Garanhir on Beltane (May Day), he was fished up by Gwyddno's son Elphin, who took him home with him, naming the boy Taliesin (He of the Fair Brow). Later, Taliesin the 'Chief of Bards' was able to return the compliment by rescuing Elphin from Maelgwn Gwynedd's castle at Deganwy (near Llandudno).

The views from this walk are truly romantic, especially in the evening, when the sun sets across the sea and illuminates the Dyfi estuary, where Taliesin was cast adrift as a baby. The actual grave has been tampered with over the years. It is recorded that when people dug into the grave in the 19th century, their action provoked a sudden thunderstorm. Leys, or earth energy lines, can be dowsed here, while the old road known as Sarn Helen passes close to Bedd Taliesin. Popularly ascribed to the Romans, who built forts along it, this is an even older trackway.

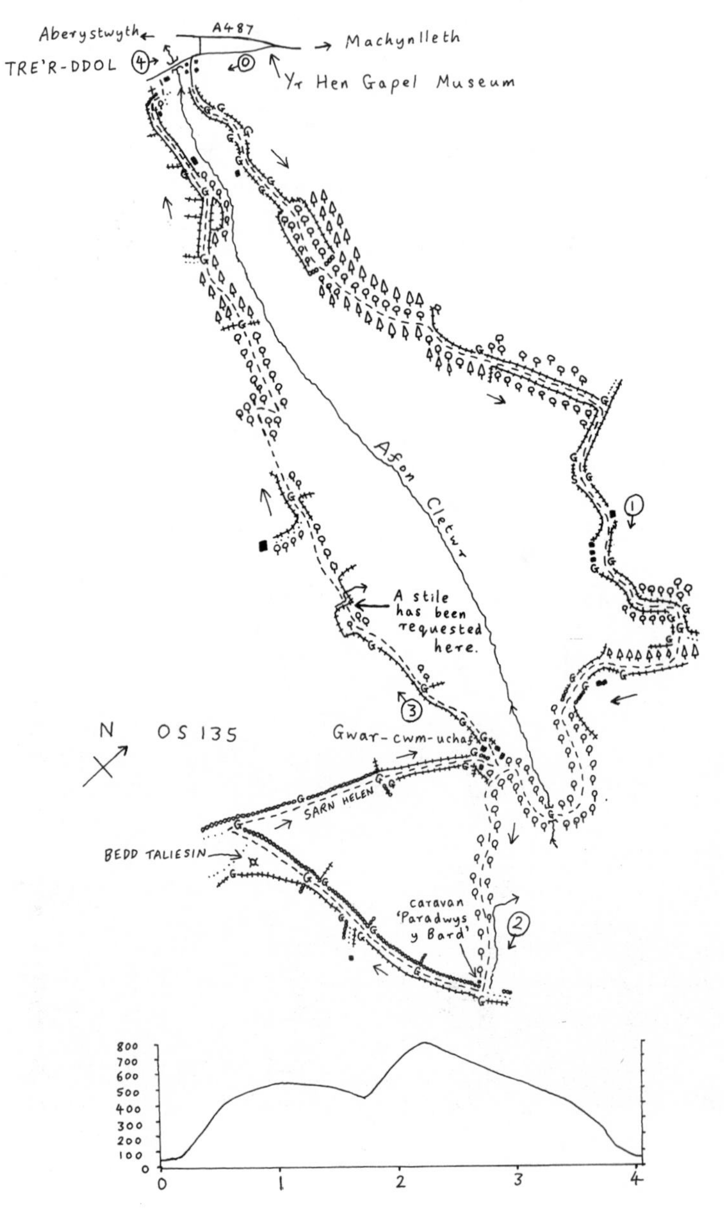
0
1/4
1/2
3/4
1
Aberystwyth
A487
Machynlleth
TRE'R-DDOL
4
0
Yr Hen Gapel Museum
Afon Cletwr
1
A stile has been requested here.
3
N
OS 135
Gwar-cwm-uchaf
SARN HELEN
BEDD TALIESIN
caravan 'Paradwys y Bard'
2
800
700
600
500
400
300
200
100
0
0
1
2
3
4

WALK DIRECTIONS

Walk past the garage and café on your right as you follow the road into the village of Tre'r-ddôl. Turn left just before the bridge along a narrow metalled lane, which soon acquires tufts of grass. Follow this lane uphill through woodland and past farm buildings to a gate across the lane. Soon after this, turn right at a junction with a similar lane and follow this across a bridge over the Afon Cletwr to reach a farm (Gwar-cwm-uchaf).

Turn left onto an old green lane which climbs up to a walled track near a caravan which is appropriately named 'Paradwys y Bard'. The view back over the Dyfi estuary is superb. Go right along the walled track, going through two gates before the fence veers away on your left and leads you to Bedd Taliesin, Taliesin's grave. Drop down to the gate on your right and walk with the wall on your left along Sarn Helen back to Gwar-cwm-uchaf. Turn sharply left to go through a gate and follow the footpath downhill to Tre'r-ddôl. Turn right across the bridge to retrace your steps to the start.

Bedd Taliesin.

8 SARN GYNFELYN

Starting Point:	Aberystwyth Railway Station, near which the buses stop.
Map Reference:	SN 585816 (O.S. Landranger sheet 135).
Distance:	6 miles.
Parking:	There is a signposted car park near the start of this walk.
Public Transport:	Couldn't be better! Buses and trains connect the start and finish of this walk, even on Sundays in winter.

Follow the waymark arrow towards Borth's war memorial, on the horizon.

This is a linear walk, but the provision of public transport (both train and bus) at each end overcomes the problem of having to get back to a parked car. The cliffs between Aberystwyth and Borth are marvellous to walk along, just as good as in Pembrokeshire. Here there is the added interest of a famous legend. Try to come when the tide is out, so that you can see Sarn Gynfelin. This is an impressive shingle ridge which extends from the shore at Wallog. It is said to be an ancient causeway leading to Cantre'r Gwaelod (Lowland Hundred). After Lyonesse, this was the largest tract of land recorded as being submerged around the British coastline.

The seas drowned it in the 6th century AD and Sarn Gynfelin ran to its principal settlement, Caer Wyddno, the city of Gwyddno Garanhir. This cultured and brave leader constructed sea walls to protect his extensive territory, but one night a gate-master, Seithenyn, was too drunk to do his duty and the sea burst through. Seithenyn's sons took holy orders in an attempt to atone for their father's negligence. Gwyddno was reducd to fishing at a salmon weir at Borth (where his son, Elphin, discovered Taliesin). A submerged forest can be seen on the beach at Borth.

Near the end of the walk, at Borth.

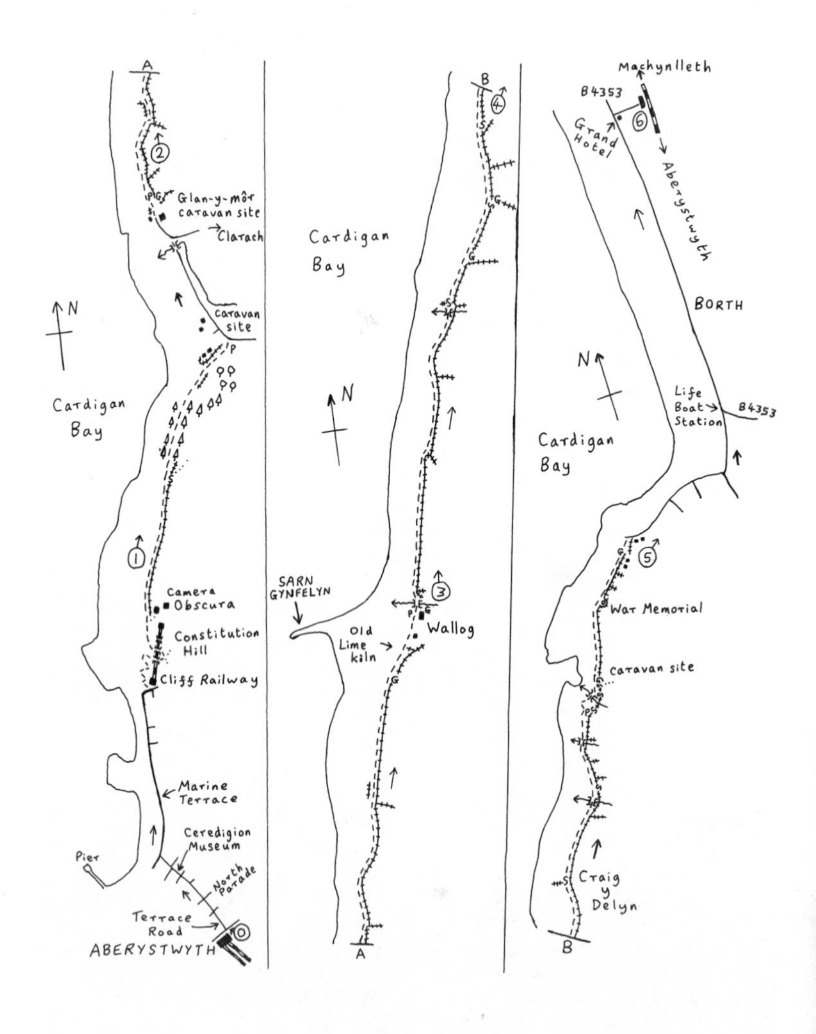
A
2
Glan-y-môr caravan site
Clarach
Caravan site
N
Cardigan Bay
1
Camera Obscura
Constitution Hill
Cliff Railway
Marine Terrace
Ceredigion Museum
North Parade
Pier
Terrace Road
0
ABERYSTWYTH
B
4
Cardigan Bay
N
SARN GYNFELYN
3
Old Lime kiln
Wallog
A
Machynlleth
B4353
6
Grand Hotel
Aberystwyth
BORTH
N
Life Boat Station
B4353
Cardigan Bay
5
War Memorial
caravan site
Craig y Delyn
B

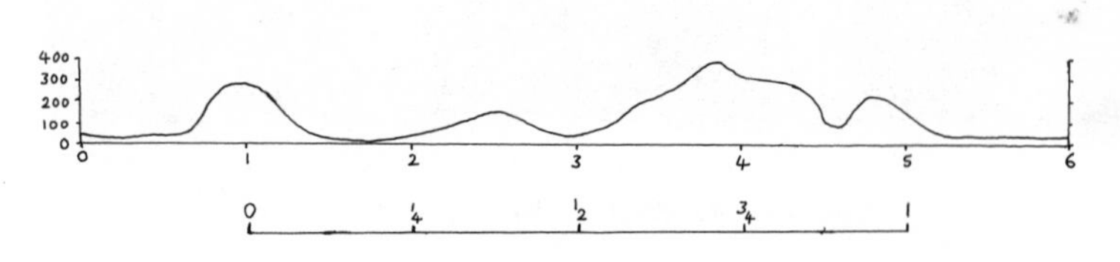
400
300
200
100
0
0
1
2
3
4
5
6
0
¼
½
¾
1

WALK DIRECTIONS

Walk up Terrace Road to reach the sea front at Aberystwyth. It is worth visiting the Ceredigion Museum along the way. This is tucked in between Boot's and Peacock's, on your right, and is open from 10 to 5 on weekdays. The only criticism of this fine museum is that it will tempt you to spend good walking time indoors. The sea breezes will soon bring the colour back to your cheeks as you turn right along Marine Terrace. From now until the end of the walk, the sea is on your left.

Climb up the zigzag path beside the Cliff Railway (or cheat and ride). While on Constitution Hill there is another recommended diversion – to the Camera Obscura. Continue the walk by following the path to the left of the café, with an old fence on your right. Keep the sea on your left and walk carefully along the cliffs. The path drops down to little bays and crosses footbridges, but it is easy to follow and well signposted. When you reach Borth, go left along the main street until the Grand Hotel on your right. Turn right for the railway station (or take a bus from the main street).

The Camera Obscura on top of Constitution Hill, Aberystwyth.

The cliff path between Aberystwyth and Borth.

One of the standing stones set in the churchyard wall at Ysbyty Cynfyn.

9 YSBYTY CYNFYN

Starting Point:	Ysbyty Cynfyn church, on the A4120 between Devil's Bridge and Ponterwyd.
Map Reference:	SN 753792 (O.S. Landranger sheet 135).
Distance:	3 miles.
Parking:	There is parking space in front of the church, but please avoid service times.
Public Transport:	The nearest bus service is from Aberystwyth to Ponterwyd (501, tel. Aberystwyth 617951 and 611085). Ponterwyd is nearly 1½ miles north of Ysbyty Cynfyn, while Devil's Bridge is nearly 2 miles to the south. There is a seasonal steam train service from Aberystwyth to Devil's Bridge, plus buses (538, 568 & 596, tel. Aberystwyth 617951 & 828288). There is a youth hostel at Ystumtuen, near the half-way point of this circular walk.

An ancient stone circle above Ysbyty Cynfyn.

This is a marvellous walk around wild, rugged country, overlooking the wooded gorge of the Rheidol, with its beautiful waterfalls. There are plenty of interesting things to see, starting with the church of St John at Ysbyty Cynfyn. The churchyard wall has five large standing stones set in it, giving rise to the claim that it was built around an old stone circle. Christian churches were, indeed, set in pagan circles and this is an old church which used to act as a hospice for pilgrims travelling to Strata Florida Abbey (Ysbyty Cynfyn is Welsh for first boundary hospital).

The tallest stone, to the far right as you stand by the churchyard gate, is probably truly ancient. It seems that the others, however, may have been incorporated into the wall in the early 19th century, when the church was rebuilt. Some of the stones actually stand above the wall's foundations, while the authentic local ancient stone circles are formed with much smaller stones.

Spend time in the churchyard to find a grave under a tree and next to the railings on the left of the church's porch. The grave is that of Isaac Hughes, who died on 6th March, 1856, aged 32 and of his son Hugh, who died on 1st March, his daughter Hannah, who died on 10th March, aged 3, and of the first recorded quadruplets, Margaret, Elizabeth, Catherine and Isaac, who all died within six days of their birth on February 17th, 1856. Only their mother, Margaret, survived that year's outbreak of typhoid.

George Borrow came this way and was urged to see 'Pont yr Offeiriad or the Parson's Bridge, because in the old time the clergyman passed over it every Sunday to do duty in the church here'. Rev. Richard Davies was known to use it in 1722 as a short cut when officiating on the same day at both Ysbyty Cynfyn and Ystumtuen. Until 1951, the bridge was just a plank hung from the sides of the gorge by chains above the Rheidol, which is a deep-cutting river. The steep slopes of its valley sides have saved the native sessile oak trees from being sacrificed to the ploughman.

A genuinely ancient circle of small standing stones is passed on the walk, as are several lead mines. A reservoir was constructed to serve Penrhiw, Bwlchgwyn and Llynteifi lead mines near Ystumtuen, while the Rheidol supplied water for the 19th century Temple Mine, named after the Knights Templar who also mined lead here in the middle ages.

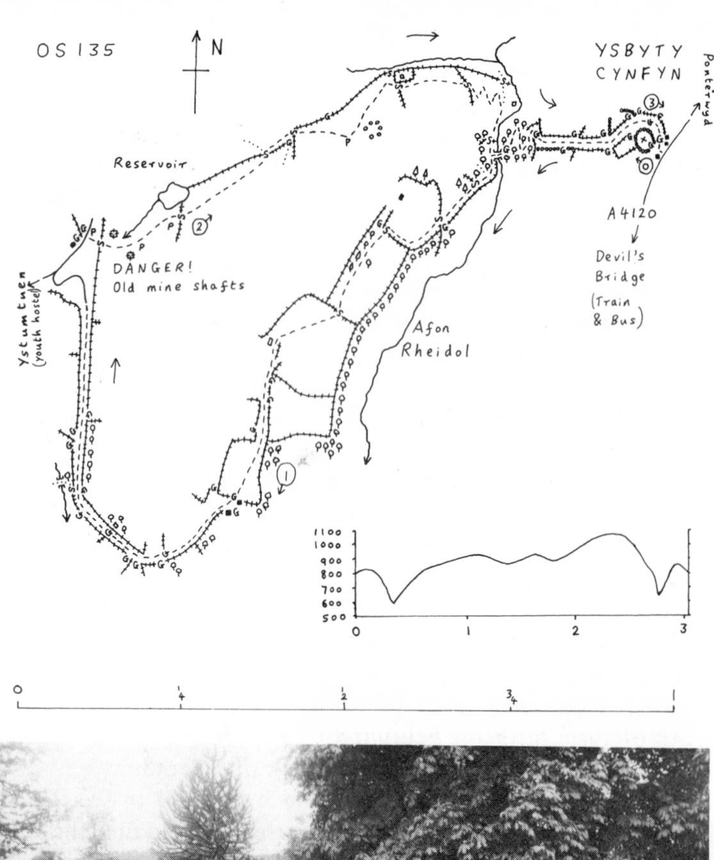

Pass through the gate to the right of the church

WALK DIRECTIONS

Pass through the gate to the right of the church. Follow the path around to the left, then ahead until you stand above a wooded valley.

Go through the gate on your right to follow a path which zigzags down through the trees to a footbridge across the river. This is Parson's Bridge and the river is the Rheidol.

Cross the footbridge, turn left and keep the fence on your left as you cross two stiles. Walk with the fence on your left around the edge of a field to a stile in the far right corner. Cross this stile and go ahead along a track to a stile. Veer right towards an old ruin after crossing this stile.

Pass the ruin on your right as you walk with a fence on your left. Cross the field to a gate giving access to a farmyard. Follow the clear track which bends right until it meets a road.

Go down to a junction with another road (which leads to Ystumtuen, where there is a youth hostel, on your left). Turn right uphill to pass a building on your left and reach a signpost on your right.

Turn right to cross a stile and follow a path uphill between two fenced and dangerous old mine shafts. Reach a stile in the fence ahead near the reservoir on your left.

Go ahead towards another stile, in the fence on your left. Cross this and keep the fence on your right until a stile ahead. Bear right downhill from this stile to a waymark post and turn left along a clear track. Notice the ancient stone circle on your right.

Cross a stile to the right of the ruin in the bottom left corner of this field and descend to a stile in the fence above the valley. Follow the path which zigzags down to join a lower path near an old mine building and turn right along it to Parson's Bridge, from where you retrace your steps to Ysbyty Cynfyn church.

The modern, safer Parson's Bridge across the river Rheidol.

Nant Dolfolau, flowing down to Garreg – ddu Reservoir, Elan Valley.

10 GARREG-DDU RESERVOIR

Starting Point:	Picnic place and car park on the eastern side of Garreg-ddu Reservoir, at its northern end, where a forestry road meets the lakeside road, opposite a gate which marks the course of the dismantled Elan Valley Railway. Look for the picnic place just before the conifer plantation on your right as you drive from Rhayader.
Map Reference:	SN 916667 (O.S. Landranger sheet 136 or 147).
Distance:	5 miles.
Parking:	There is a car park at the start.
Public Transport:	None.

An old Elan Valley Railway bridge across Nant Dolfolau as it flows into Garreg-ddu Reservoir.

The Elan Valley is the Lake District of Mid Wales. Its lakes are reservoirs, but they are far too picturesque to be saddled with that label. Birmingham Corporation was responsible for building the dams around 1900, when the manufacturing heart of the British empire needed to look to Wales for its water supply. A railway was built to enable the dams to be constructed and this walk starts along the bed of this dismantled track before climbing up to the deserted plateau, where ancient monuments stand witness to an earlier population when the sessile oaks, whose branches still shade part of our route, were the predominant vegetation.

The view of Penygarreg Reservoir from the descending moorland path near the end of this walk.

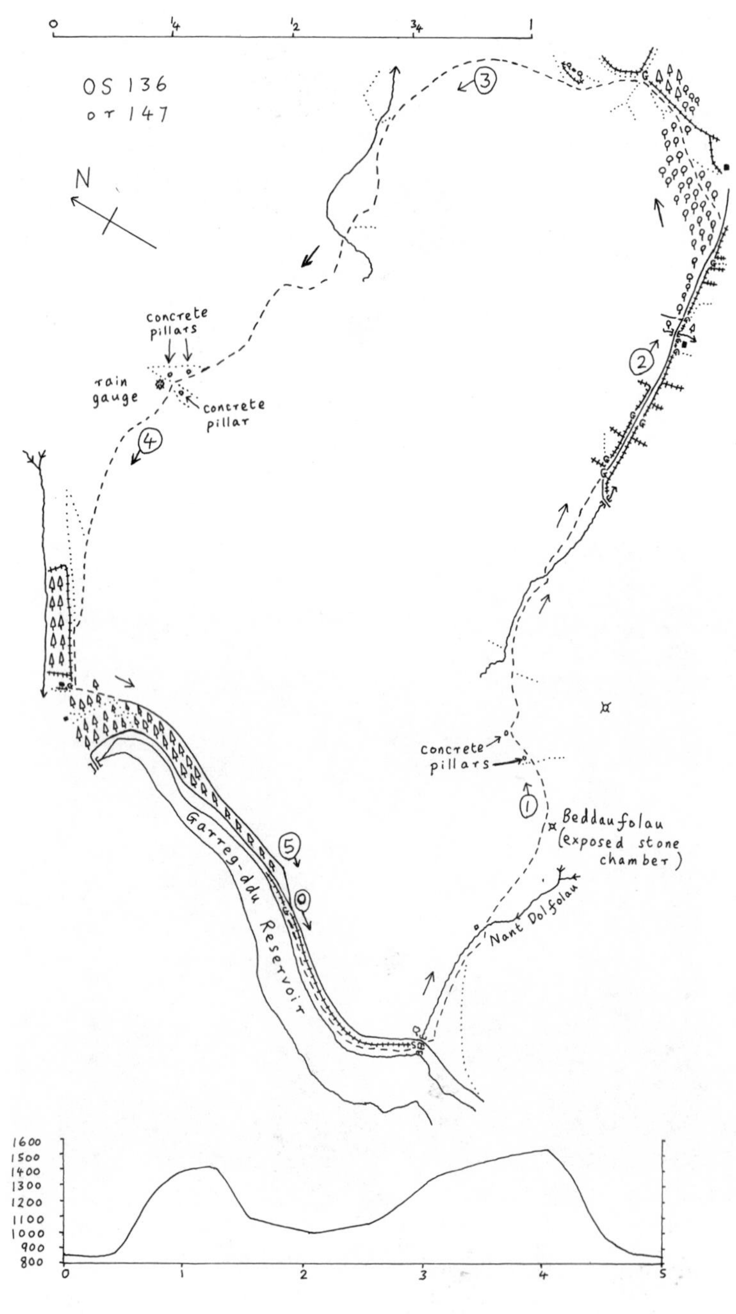
0
1/4
1/2
3/4
1
OS 136
or 147
N
3
2
concrete
pillars
rain
gauge
concrete
pillar
4
concrete
pillars
1
Beddaufolau
(exposed stone
chamber)
Nant Dolfolau
5
0
Garreg-ddu Reservoir
1600
1500
1400
1300
1200
1100
1000
900
800
0
1
2
3
4
5

WALK DIRECTIONS

Cross the road to a gate which gives access to the dismantled railway track and walk along this with Garreg-ddu Reservoir on your right until you meet an old railway bridge. Turn left over a stile and turn right along the road across a bridge, then turn left to walk upstream with Nant Dolfolau on your left. Cross this stream near a ruin and keep to the path which eventually meets another stream on your left, crosses it and goes downstream to a lane, which is followed until a path bears left through oak trees.

Pass conifers on your right and veer left, uphill, along a clear track. Keep climbing with this track to cross a stream and reach a crosstracks near a fenced-in rain gauge. Go ahead to see Penygarreg Reservoir on your right as you descend to conifer trees and bear left along the forest track to descend gradually to the picnic place at the start of the walk.

Your path through the oak trees.

11 CABAN-COCH RESERVOIR

Starting Point:	Elan Valley Visitor Centre, reached down a slip road on your left, as you come from Rhayader, at the end of the B4518. It is signposted.
Map Reference:	SN 928647 (O.S. Landranger sheet 147).
Distance:	8½ miles (n.b. the last half mile is distorted on the map in order to fit the space available).
Parking:	There is a car park at the Visitor Centre.
Public Transport:	Bus from Rhayader on Wednesdays (tel. Penybont 207 for current times).

Looking across the southern end of Caban-coch Reservoir.

The Elan Valley Visitor Centre makes a fine introduction to this beautiful part of Mid Wales. Impressive statistics abound about the total storage capacity of the five reservoirs (22,000 million gallons) and of the gallons per day that flow by gravity to the English Midlands (76 million). Set out on this walk to discover what is most impressive about the Elan Valley, however – its superb scenery, coupled with a sense of freedom given by the lack of human population and the presence of red kite, buzzards and other birds.

This walk takes you right round one of the lakes (how could it be termed a reservoir, when it fits into the landscape so well?). A clear track takes you along the lakeside, then up above the trees for some fine views from an altitude of 1400 feet. The southern end of Caban-coch Reservoir is rounded and Afon Claerwen, the tributary of the Elan which helps to feed this reservoir is crossed. The valley side is climbed again to reach a forest track which takes you to Nantgwllt church before the road is followed back to the Visitor Centre.

Caban-coch Reservoir seen from above the trees on the outward track.

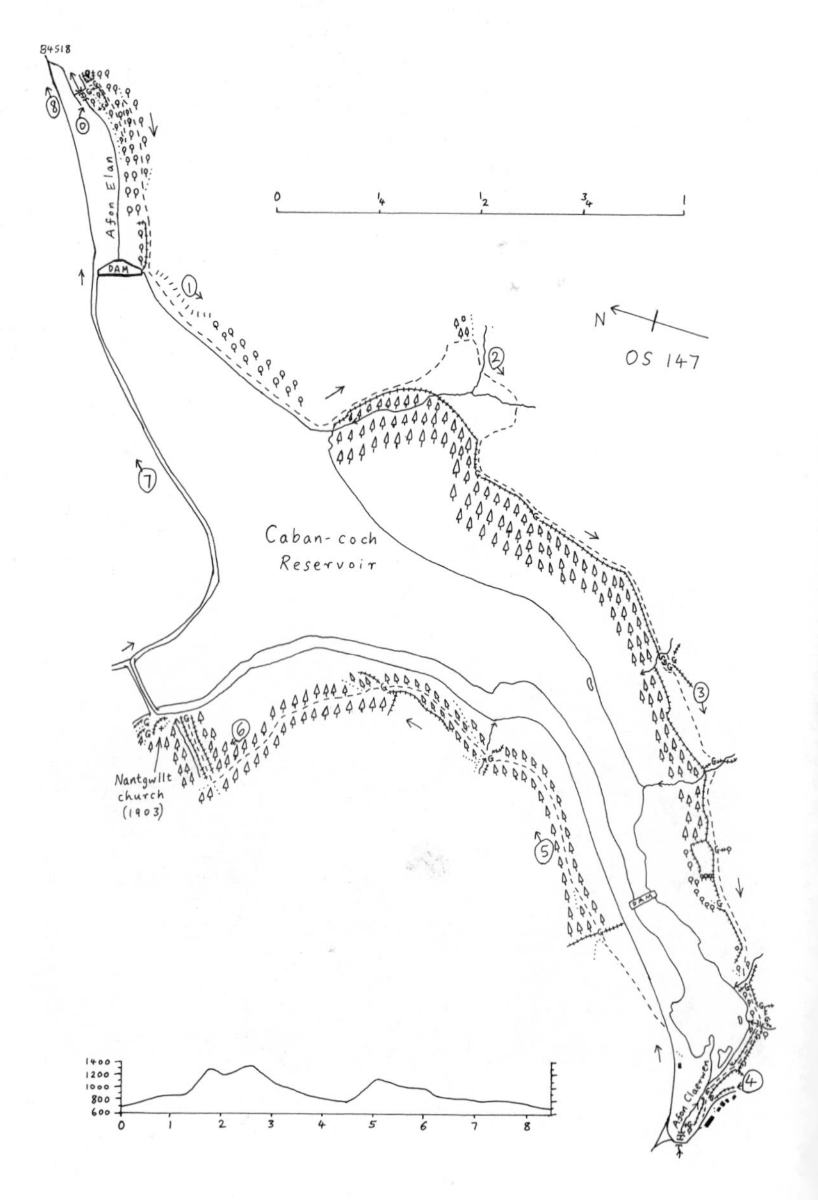
B4518
Afon Elan
DAM
0
1/4
1/2
3/4
1
N
OS 147
Caban-coch
Reservoir
Nantgwllt
church
(1903)
DAM
Afon Claerwen
1400
1200
1000
800
600
0
1
2
3
4
5
6
7
8

WALK DIRECTIONS

Go back to the entrance to the Elan Valley Visitor Centre and turn right across the safer of the two bridge across the Afon Elan. The road turns left, but you go straight ahead through a gate (n.b. not through a side gate on your right) and follow the path through the oak trees on your right. Turn sharply left to zigzag uphill, turning right to reach the dam on your right. Go left to walk with the lake on your right until you come to a conifer plantation where you bear left uphill. Trees mark an old ruin where you turn right along a clear track which is followed until the southern end of the lake on your right.

Follow a road across the Afon Claerwen and turn right at a telephone box. Look for a clear track going uphill on your left and follow it into a forest. Go ahead along a forestry track until a crosstracks where you turn right down a fenced track to reach the road. Go left to visit Nantgwllt church, then follow the road between two reservoirs (Caban-coch and Garreg-ddu). Turn right on the other side to follow the road back to the Visitor Centre.

The clear track above the trees and Caban-coch reservoir, on your right.

Two views of the southern end of Caban-coch Reservoir.

Maen-serth

12 NANT GWYNLLYN

Starting Point:	St Winifred's Church, Llansantffraed-Cwmdeuddwr, which is just across the bridge over the river Wye to the west of Rhayader.
Map Reference:	SN 968677 (O.S. Landranger sheet 136 or 147).
Distance:	7 miles.
Parking:	There are parking spaces near the church (but please avoid service times).
Public Transport:	Buses run to Rhayader from Llandrindod (nearest British Rail station), Builth Wells, Llanwrtyd, Aberystwyth and Hereford (tel. Penybont 207 and Rhayader 810791 for current days and times).

Go through this gate into the forest.

The high plateau west of Rhayader is splendid walking country. It is even possible to walk through remnants of the original sessile oak forest, while ancient monuments remind us of the great age of these paths. St Winifred's is the modern name of the church at the start of this walk, but it was originally dedicated to St Bridget, or Bride, whose name comes from the Sanskrit 'Braht' (the exalted one). A feast was traditionally held here every February, which was the time of the pagan feast of Imbolc, dedicated to Bride. Christianity is long-established here, however, as the stone christening font in the church porch dates from the 5th century.

The highlight of the walk is the series of waterfalls along Nant Gwynllyn. The broad upland track which leads back to Rhayader could tell many a tale, however. It passes Maen-serth, a prominent standing stone at 1500 feet. Look for a rough cross engraved on it. This is a memorial to Einion Clud, the native Welsh chieftain of Elvel, who was murdered here by the Normans in the 12th century (the stone is much older, of course, and seems to mark a ley, or earth energy line).

Follow this old road from Maen-serth down towards Rhayader.

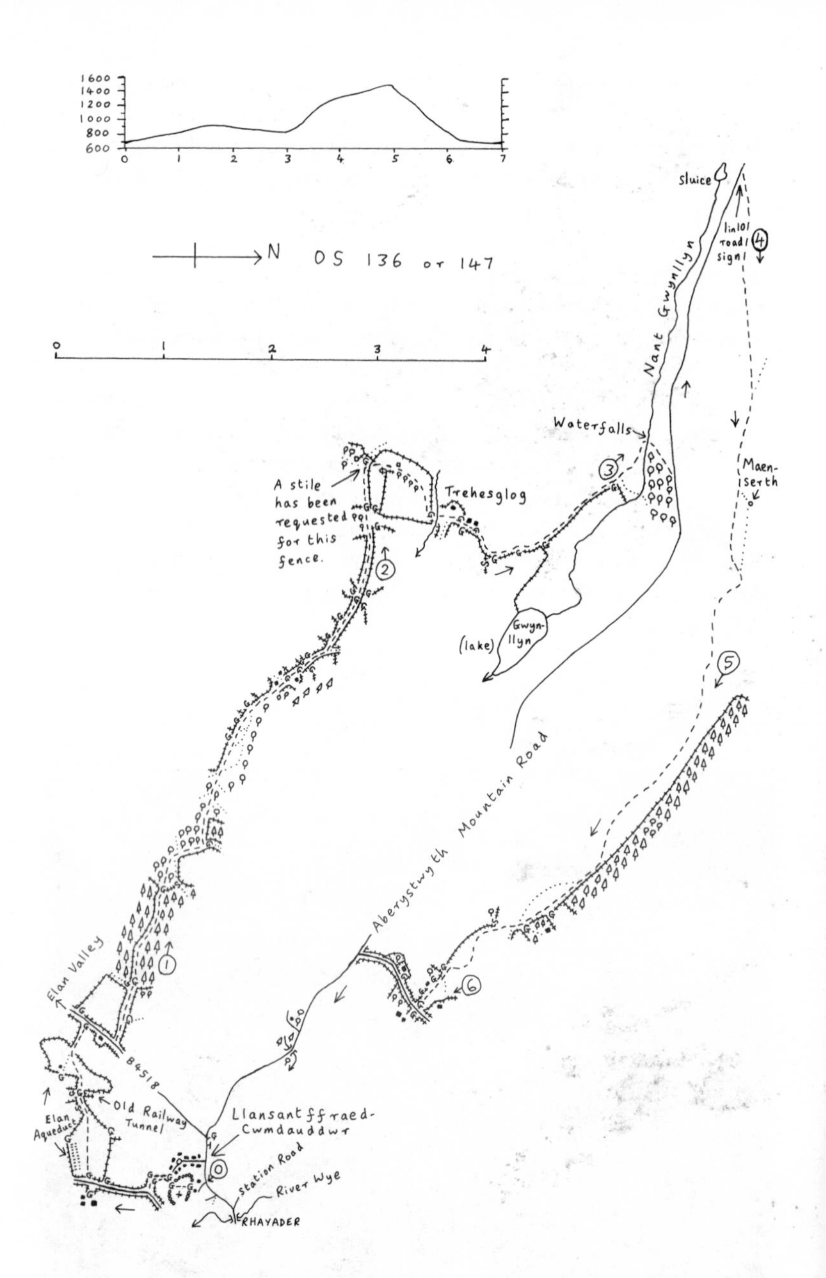
1600
1400
1200
1000
800
600
0
1
2
3
4
5
6
7
N
OS 136 or 147
0
1
2
3
4
Sluice
1in10 road sign
4
Nant Gwynllyn
Waterfalls
3
Maen-serth
A stile has been requested for this fence.
Trehesglog
2
Gwyn-llyn
(lake)
5
Aberystwyth Mountain Road
1
Elan Valley
6
B4518
Old Railway Tunnel
Elan Aqueduct
Llansantffraed-Cwmdauddwr
0
Station Road
River Wye
RHAYADER

WALK DIRECTIONS

Go through the churchyard and continue up a field to a gate and turn left to a lane. Go right until the second gate on your right, where you turn to cross a field and bear left along a fenced track over the old Mid Wales Railway tunnel (the line ran from Talyllyn Junction, near Brecon, to Moat Lane Junction, near Caersws). Continue to the B4518 and turn right along this road until a hedged track on your left, which leads you to a forest. Keep to the main path through the forest to reach a farm. Go ahead along its access track until an old green lane bears left. Turn right at its end and follow a path through Trehesglog to reach Nant Gwynllyn and its waterfalls. Cross the stream and walk up to the Aberystwyth mountain road, where you turn left uphill.

Turn right at a '1 in 10' road sign to follow a moorland track. Notice Maen-serth on your left before the track descends towards Rhayader. Turn right along a lane to reach the Aberystwyth mountain road, which you turn left along to reach the B4518 and keep left to reach the church, which is now on your right.

Follow this path through the oak forest.

KEY TO THE MAPS

Symbol	Meaning
3	The footpath route with distance walked from the start in miles and direction of walk.
	Other path (not necessarily right of way)
	Motor road
	Railway line
	Hedge or fence
	Wall
	Standing stone
	Stone circle
G	Gate
S	Stile
P	Signpost
	Stream or river with direction of flow
	Bridge
	Elan Valley Aqueduct (buried)
¤	Tumulus
	Campsite
	Steep, dangerous crags
	Trees
	Buildings
	Ruin
+	Church or chapel
N	Direction of north (which may not always be at the top of the map).
OS 135	Relevant Ordnance Survey Landranger sheet

Each map has a scale in miles, which varies from map to map.
Each map has a gradient profile showing the height in feet above sea level and the distance in miles from the start.
Afon is Welsh for river, nant means stream.